DISPLACEMENT

DISPLACEMENT

Leslie Harrison

A Mariner Original / Mariner Books
HOUGHTON MIFFLIN HARCOURT
Boston   New York   2009

Copyright © 2009 by Leslie Harrison

Foreword copyright © 2009 by Eavan Boland

For information about permission to reproduce selections
from this book, write to Permissions, Houghton Mifflin
Harcourt Publishing Company, 215 Park Avenue South,
New York, New York 10003.

www.hmhbooks.com

Library of Congress Cataloging-in-Publication Data
Harrison, Leslie, date
   Displacement / Leslie Harrison.
      p. cm.
   "A Mariner Original."
   ISBN 978-0-547-19842-2
   1. Displacement (Psychology) — Poetry. 2. Loss
(Psychology) — Poetry. I. Title.
   PS3608.A78357D57 2009
   811'.6—dc22   2008053288

Book design by Melissa Lotfy

Printed in the United States of America

DOC 10 9 8 7 6 5 4 3 2 1

For my families — the one I was born into, the ones I've made

And for my mother, Eleanor Railsback (1934–2008)
and my grandmother, Marion Cook (1913–2009)

Contents

Foreword

Leslie Harrison's book has the evocative title *Displacement*. But not far into these poems, the reader finds the strength of the theme lies in its unsettling lack of definition. What exactly is being displaced? The body? The mind? The landscape?

In many of the lyric poems here the answer seems to be all of them: that unless one of them has poise, none of them will. The one element that is not displaced—that plants its step and holds its ground—is poetic voice. It rings out, modulates, goes high and low and convinces from start to finish. It is capable of rhetoric, of down-to-earth vernacular; it has a gift for soliloquy and a weakness for monologue, as every human voice does. And listening to it is much like listening to a powerful, self-directed conversation. Much of the charm and music of this book for me—and I believe for other readers—must have to do with this unabashed contradiction between a voice that has found its place in the poem, and a life that will not find an equivalent ease in the world.

The clearest example of this is also one of the most inviting poems in the book—"The Day Beauty Divorced Meaning." I will quote it whole, since it is a poem of unusual wholeness, and also of visible, engaging contradictions: It has a sonnet mood, but is not a sonnet. It has a tone of irony, but is not ironic. It is, like so much of the fine writing here, a coalition of opposites: a lament for a life's occasion articulated through a zest for language.

Their friends looked shocked—said *not
possible*, said *how sad*. The trees carried on
with their treeish lives—stately except when
they shed their silly dandruff of birds. And
the ocean did what oceans mostly do—

suspended almost everything, dropped one
small ship, or two. The day beauty divorced
meaning, someone picked a flower, a fight,
a flight. Someone got on a boat.
A closet lost its suitcases. Someone
was snowed in, someone else on. The sun
went down and all it was, was night.

I often think not enough is made of the way tone guides, waylays,
and finally decides on the destination of the poem it appears to serve.
It is a dominant Ariel, questioning and resisting and confusing the
otherwise clear path. This is as true of a poem like "Tea," which med-
itates on the small ritual of drinking it to the mythic sequence that
opens the books where Pasiphaë, Daedalus, and the Minotaur pro-
vide costumes for dark themes of erotic loyalty and betrayal. This is a
book with a real understanding of tone — its reliable scale, its durable
music.

I could list a number of other poems that caught my eye. There
is, for instance, "Pantoum for a Walk in the Woods" and the playful,
deceptive poem called "Past Tense," which uses all the registers of
tone, language, and fractured syntax to lure the reader into the laby-
rinth. The following lines open the poem:

Was fired — on fire, not absent from pay
Was burning, was being fire over water
Was ashes, ashes. Was all fall down.
Was dusted was lusted. Was lusted after
Was flower'd. Not de- too late for that
Was leafed and green was left
Was left after — long — the altar
Was altered, leaning far out of true
Was pitched was pitched wrong, and also out.

But excerpts, and even entire examples, are never the same as the book itself. There is a poise and presence about this book—and a poignance about its traffic between secrecy and disclosure—that allow it to have unusual force, and a true grip on its reader. This is a real lyric journey; and the reader will take it too.

EAVAN BOLAND

The Four Elements

I. Pasiphaë

Wife: word and vow. Invisible. Bound —
as heat is to flame. No god did this,
no pretty, facile cow. A kingdom
of men, blinded. And me — burning
to be seen. Burning for him. I chose,
did not haggle over price. At last,
in the ashes, after, you see me.

I made sure his whores spewed only
monsters. And I am one of them.

II. Daedalus

Falling, all my life. Not clever enough
not to come between a king, his wife.
No map for how to live past this.
I dismantled sleep, built wings, became
the air, took what I loved — rescued him.
But not to keep.

III. The Minotaur

I was a monster. I knew. At home
in the stone prison, innocent, amazed,
I simply was. But then they came —
fair and afraid. I looked, held them in
my gaze, saw it in their eyes: the other.
A monster. Me. Devoured what they had taught:

beauty. Became its absence. Lay down
in welcoming mud, offered up
my misborn head. Took the blows. Was glad.

IV. Icarus

Pick up that shell. Hold it to your ear.
It is not the sea that sings inside,
not beating waves you hear. It is me —
rinsed of ash, earth, and air; no architect,
ant, or string as guide — lost. And drowning.

I carried them all, tried to set them free.
Burned her away in the sun, wore cloud,
escaped the walls, was lovely for them,
but fell for me.

I.

PASIPHAË

Firefly

1.

The bats at dusk: their wild aerial twitch
and slide and all the while the moon

is underground — not quite silvering
the edges yet — and you at the door.

My attention is given too often
to the sky, you say. I pretend

I can't hear through the screen —
a thin net that holds

not even the light inside.

2.

I nearly drowned once, or that's
the way you tell the story.

But what I learned was how lovely
the inside of a river is — champagne

cascade of bubbles, fizzy clatter
of small stones tumbling along

the bottom, the beachglass color
of the place, the two directions —

air and forward—and the shine
that is the wrong side of surface—

that shine—the breaking of it.

3.

Asleep, my body turns
away from you. For years, I fear

I will go on sleeping
curled at the edge of every bed.

4.

I wake and want bitter black tea
and solitude so much I think

my dreams must be as crowded
as the firefly meadow, as the bed

the river made.

5.

The bats again: not just mosquitoes,
but also the fireflies' glow—desire's

neon sign. In the meadow, mated
or eaten, the lights grow few, go out.

Fifty States: A Travelogue (I)

The World

A three-chambered heart
through which the river flows:
the dark ground welling,
the bright sky broken,
the folded, anonymous ocean.

The Arctic

When the cointoss came,
the land that winter elected to defend.

Darkness

What if you love the night,
the simplifying of it—
a limited palette explaining
your life in shades
of silver and midnight?

Dawn

Black turns to blue under the weight
of falling bodies.

Morning

It is the job of the light to send us back again,
cast us hard into our own bodies
as caught fish are flung.

The Woods

A beauty that costs only absence,
strong flesh, the recoverable sting
of small feeding things,

the plain moments—unadorned—
easy to mistake for peace.

Home —as hiking

Though in theory night happens first to the sky,
when you are idling worn boots in a pond

tucked just below the summit, when you are watching
a beaver navigate and chew, stroke and fell,

when you are watching this still pool, this creature,
these winded trees, then night is a thing that happens

first behind your back. The sky thins and sheens.
Darkness fills a valley scattered with stars,

one of which you live in.

2.

I get as far as the rise edging the yard;
the trees behind beckon like a jailbreak.
But I sit and watch the risen dark sliced

by spill of yellow light, the window making
of the night an architecture—his shadow
pacing the bright aquarium that dusk has made.

And overhead, the stars

3.

have done what I have done—have spent the day
spinning and whirling beyond sight, unhoused
and absent—meaningless. But now, the night

complete, the stars and I assemble in
our usual places, shining, as always,
in a litany of fresh and ancient betrayals.

I Dream of Rain

Your eyes look like the river, he said, hand
slack and shadowed in the truck, radio channeling

NPR, glitter of silver scales like mica
a dried bright smear across one cheek. I

slid damp back down the vinyl bench,
slid eyes up at the schooling swirl of branches

passing in the wake of what movement we muster
and pondered the past-tense fate of mouths,

volcanoes, stains—all evidence of aperture and the sly
habits of liquids, evidence also of the lies

in words, his hands. I thought of the snapped spine
of the fish, casual swipe with scale-stained hand

at a mosquito—artist of drawn blood, drawn breath.
They account, he had said, for one of every sixteen deaths,

and I thought for a second he meant his hands,
but he meant the insect he missed intent instead on

killing the fish that, hungry and alive, would have
devoured the subject. Dizzy with the march of branch

and road, sunflicker promising migraine later, sweater thin
like the wings of a moth pinned by a sudden rain,

I remembered the slick stretch, the sick fight
of both river and trout against the hook, his line.

Solstice

Today light runs counter to the season.
Dwindle begins as summer does.

The monarch is bitter with the weedy milk
and his endless, vacant nations.

This is the address of distance,
where distance came to live

in the seefar longlight in the shining day.

Later the storms grumble past
dropping intimations on their way to the sea.

Moon lanterns late lake as if
either had ever been possessed of light.

I'm sorry for your loss I say
to the moon, all hungerbelly and short flight.

This is the entrance to the museum of darkness.

On the hillside, the curated dead
are on permanent loan to the museum of cold.

How It Started

At the point you start throwing pebbles
at large bodies of water, you have suffered
an error of judgment. Or scale.

Marriage kept sending me back.
To the river. The edge of it. Sometimes hemmed
in shards of ice, sometimes rock.
The water was cold and pushed
at the shore. At the house I kept
setting the table. Knives for the dominant
hand, his grandmother's plates
in the middle of everything.

Despite the cold, the lack
of encouragement, several leaves
persisted on the box elder.

In the attic I found a mouse—spine snapped
in a trap, flesh faded to a faint smell
at the very edge of things. Loosed
from the broken bones—a fine
rice of white infant skulls.

When he found the limp
indigo bundle of a bird on his plate,
I blamed the cat.

When I told him about the mouse
he reset the trap.

The Spider

Sitting under the skylight, which plays
a badly tuned song of summer rain,
I watch a spider on the lampshade.

It waves front legs over each pleated
precipice, navigates lit ravines,
does or does not discern the polite

Swedish plaid of yellow, white, and blue.
I lean closer, and the spider
curls itself into a defensive

oval knot. Overhead, the pigeons
slap the air with a sound like trying
to make a newborn breathe. The spider

uncurls and narrows another gap
anchoring a thin strand to the lamp
in a house shaped like shattering.

I think my problem is—

that I want to live on earth as I do
in my head. Days when I have
no skin and the exchange rages
until, like mist rising from the lake,
the boundaries grow indistinct
in a haze of molecular fire.

And those days I lean
like paintings gilt-framed in language
against the walls of all the days
I cannot find a hammer, hanger, ruler.
And it does not matter—
the walls are stone and may not be adorned.

Fifty States: A Travelogue (II)

Paradise

> Highland state, clear views of Hell
> across careful walls encircling orchards
> never in flower, always in fruit.
>
> *First rule:* You are forever
> at the border, attempting entry. One way
> involves pushing body against body,
> the scent of berries rotting on the ground.
>
> *Second rule:* You will only recognize it
> as a wavering glimpse that dwindles
> small and reversed in a rearview mirror.
>
> *Third rule:* If you are not already,
> you will be the leaf, cast off,
> spent, sent from the garden.

Bodies

> *In motion:*
> All day, I throw
> my body at the mountain.
>
> *At rest:*
> At night, he says,
> I sleep like a stone.

Mount Olympus

> Terrain mountainous.
> Sturdy shoes and clothes recommended.
> Travelers take care:
> The dictionary here translates human
> as fragile, as plaything, but not rare.

Geography

> If you do not walk the land, it travels
> away from you, waits in the dark cave
> where dream and memory
> negotiate.

Conception

> Once I was this small:
> what my parents gave me
> was not enough to crowd
> any angel from the dancefloor.

Growth

> What I required then
> was division. Was water.

Autobiography —as a vase

Like porcelain thrown before birth—
both shattered and sensing the glue.

Complete, but already crazed with breaking.
Someone polishes it on the mantel.

Someone is trying to put it back
together. Someone is watching

it fall. Someone was the hand,
the air. Someone is the moment

when damaged is a fact but the shape
remains. Someone is that sudden

injection of space, that collapse. Someone
is the pieces, the dustpan, the glue.

Someone is the worklight, the patience,
the room. Someone meant for this to happen.

Someone has to decide: repair or dismiss.
It happens all at once. It happens forever.

In this story you can be everything
and everyone except unbroken.

II.

DAEDALUS

Lunar Eclipse, Baltimore

Not like a breaker trips—all at once, a sudden plunge
but rather a more subtle theft—words I'd written
falling from your mouth.

Cities squander so much light that I sit reading in the garden
aglow with excess and the lucent pulse of moth wings.
They ought to live longer here—

no need for one annealing fire with the entire city ablaze.
I'm as hollow as downtown. Shadows, freed from their objects,
gather in the cryptic chainmail sky.

The hammock moon, curved around absence, is re-created whole
in earth's dark wake—a month of vanishing compressed.
Tonight, I will dream of you,

this book, and this city. And sleep will transpose all of us
into a different tense. I will wake to a sky emptied
of the missing moon and the moths.

Fifty States: A Travelogue (III)

Firefly

> Where desire ignites the nights
> so naked and wild, blazing and erratic,
> even strangers gasp and stare,
> cannot look away.

Pure Will

> In the deceptive sun of June,
> skin torched by mosquitoes, I focus all I have
> on calling up the night. It always works,
> though sometimes it takes hours.

Dream

> Inside some foggy version
> of Venice or Baltimore
> we meet and fuck. Sometimes,
> more erotic, we simply touch. Day breaks us
> like horses, like mirrors, like guns.

Beloved

> *How do you know this is a dream?*
> If it were not, we would not.

Coupled State

He and I have both been here,
though at different times,
with other people.

Grace

The state before the state of waking,
brief moments at dawn when you believe
in other beds, lost possibilities,
before you don your life like a B movie,
unlovely and badly cut.

Longing

Contiguous to all other states.
Leave all you love with customs.
Flights depart only to the island nations,
only at night, only in November.

Huntley Meadows, May

Shadows angle
across sunsilvered wood,
the quiet scratch

of sneakers trace
the curve of boardwalk,
gray snake, arch

of gray log, the ice
clear sky fallen —
tangled in pickerel rush

matting in a tepid breeze.
Salt filters upriver like
the ache of distance

coming, and then
already here. Our hands
hold artifacts — our separate

instruments — his
to bring them closer,
mine to hold them still.

In shining marshgrass spikes,
white bird — bentmetal
rustlegs on slivered

stickwood—spreads
inverse arch of white
wings, and in that thrust,

the words have lost
their things. Referents
dissolve in early air.

Egret he says,
but that is not
what I hear.

Fable

The witch asked for my heart
as proof and I asked the river
about deceit. Also sleep.

That night, the woods locked
behind new-moon gates
of blindness, the river replied:

She doesn't want your blood,
white-warm child, she wants it
stopped, dammed, damned,

the pump shut down. The witch
whispered back—*the only thing
a river knows is going.*

Farming the Moon

Driving north on 83, end of May,
we are going home. Crammed full, weighed
down with words, your truck creeps
up the grades, hesitates. Tears push the grit
of moving aside in streams the highway breeze

turns dry. Migrating birds outline the wind.
At home, unpacked, colder still in June,
I keep finding a layer of dust
from Baltimore that coats my books the way
the city abrades my dreams. I cannot keep

my balance. Gravity inverts, then seeps
through ears and feet. A seesaw sun
arcs through each day, gains weight
as it eats the margins of July.
The meteors that strike the moon break rocks

to ever smaller bits. This powdered regolith
forms lakes. Like Sperry Pond, they're deep
enough to swim. It's August,
and this is called farming the moon.
Something in me is missing, and so I wait

to see what swims ashore. On tape, Tom Waits
shivers in the sea. I walk the granite
hills, striking flakes like stars
from stone, guided by the scars that sweep
across the face of fall. It is September,

a month the passing year brought back, the way
asleep, I dream a city trapped beneath
the broken, glittering stone in the sky.

Correspondence

I write you letters — in my head mostly —
as I hike, pretending I am lost.

Sometimes they make it all the way
onto paper. What they contain

is nothing much: how the Cold River,
along the road from New Hampshire

in the bitter chill, looked like jade
just as you once said.

I mention the crack of frozen trees
in the whip of a blown ravine;

how hoarfrost coats everything
at a certain height; a hawk threading

iced branches like weaving;
the way last fall the beaver's

head cut the water into a spreading V,
how at the apex its teeth

curve in, toward the heart,
how they glow in the peat

tinted water; the way I dream
you in a city I couldn't keep;

how in Japan they leash
cormorants, then let them fish

for carp to feed an emperor;
how maps fill my head—a metaphor

no doubt. The Japanese also
have a word—*mujo*—

for the terrible transience of things:
water on a leashed bird's wing,

the smell of frost, and rivers that run
so green under this northern winter sun.

Fire

—as cliché

How not to think in the same old terms—
you as some kind of flame, some kind of heat.
Little else would suffice for the hunger,
the night stacks of words so much tinder, tender fuel.

The towns of my days: town of the treestorm,
town of the dog walkers, three-bedroom ranches,
town of Sunday papers, spring leaf burning—
so many secret perfumes—inhaled, relocated.

—as history

After it all died back, burned down,
went underground—after that,
I went to where there was no water.
I moved to the desert.

—as icon

I wanted to go to that place in Australia,
that mountain afire so long no one knows
how it started—seam of coal, steaming scar,
even a six-thousand-year-old fire
is better than extinction.

Or Centralia—town wrapped
in detours and snowmelt—a fire begun
before my birth, burning still. No one
would expect me to fight that.

A Thousand Miles

I've checked the atlas, it's a thousand miles
across most of two seasons, though quite warm
for December. It's hotter there I'm sure, no harm
in talking of the weather. Cold rain files

the ice away with the faintest rasp and creak
like sandpaper on the wood I smooth and soften.
I think of you, but won't admit how often—
no matter. The wood's swirling darker streaks

are the hurried, hard growth of spring. I sand
with the wider, summer grain. It's pale
and soft, and thins to vanish in late fall.
Dovetail joints, like fingers linking hands,

are strong all ways but one. I'm careful here
to fit them in—they're tight and need no glue.
It's a gift, a metaphor we'll both see through—
this empty box, the winters hidden there.

Fragments — on hiking

1.

In a place where trout lilies
dream a garden,
every drop of migrating blood
dreams the pump,
which for the length of the dream
is just a pump.

2.

From the high stone summit
I could fold our home
in half—like a postcard—
carry it in a pocket,
sail it off the edge
of the flat, flat world.

3.

And above—the sky like some
porcelain cup
crazed and limned,
the force of water
stilled in a scrim of thinnest,
manageable white.

4.

Vessels, unreinforced,
often collapse

under the weight
of what they contain.
See: amber, airplane, river;
see: sediment, language.

5.

At dusk, at Sperry Pond,
the stars on black water
look like stubble
through dirt
or skin, like salt
on a wound.

6.

Cold and night are simple
gestures of geography.
Windows are the myth
of clarity. By night
they are a mirror; by day
birds are broken there.

7.

Animals become
extinct from the edges
inward, leaving last
their truest home.
In us—if anything—
the opposite.

8.

As much a stranger here,
I achieve nativity
the way that stones in the city
acquire jobs: seeping
the sound of praise, rafting traffic,
anchoring the dead.

9.

Waking, the mind tangles
on the branching border, trail,
trial of sleep, of after
and before. At dawn—footprints
in new snow. Last night
the deer were at the door.

10.

Carrying you as memory,
I need that much stone
underfoot.

The Old Schoolhouse

The gray slate chalkboards rain dust, reign dusty
and afternoon stirs fragments through the air
grown stale and thicker now.
There's only you to see, and if somewhere
in the building, stray words were gathered,
assembled, and shelved — modest

and eaten — no one will read them, be improved,
make repairs. Instead you nudge the vacuum
into collection, revision.
Don't you wish you could change something? The sun
will rise again tomorrow, will torch the unloved
dust. But lately you've weathered

a different storm, and that mechanical swirl
and all your impulses conspire. What use
is the dancing, ridden swell,
this silent, narrow hall? Today this house
is empty, a series of abandoned rooms
you lived in once and believed you understood.

Dusting

This morning a dusting of snow this morning

twittering flakes flakes clumping convocations

of them on the lawn sun winter pale sideways

without force lacking a certain substance if he died

where he lives no one would think to tell me

not right away my father gone into the long

raveling of sidereal years was gone into coffin

three days before someone remembered he had

children somewhere and like the milky way

finally arriving overhead called me and absence

was made flesh and brought low into ground

though none of his children know where

this thin snow comes fragments of the cold

cold stars and somewhere he wakes or does not

and in this white dusting he like the starlight the snow

stubborn resisting dissolution continues for now

to shine

Fifty States: A Travelogue (IV)

Ophelia

> Sorrow's pool, sparrow's tool—
> beaked, branched, brown, and drowning
> —but beautifully. That's
> the point, isn't it?

Migraine

> Hours spent tucked
> under an egret's wing—
> everything frail and thunderous
> feathered and beating.

Betrayal

> One long shore
> constantly excusing the ocean.

Divorce

> No one chooses, believes they'll come here.
> But half of all marriages end in divorce, and
> every marriage involves at least two people.

November

> One last hike before I go.
> Thinly dressed in the snow,
> I dare the deep ravine, find chickadees

who live by letting parts go cold,
throw rocks at Sperry Pond, and know
it will be months before they fall.

Travel

Who on earth would carry
so much baggage?

Someone who intended to stay.

Hoarfrost

Dawn: Ground fog gathers and unfurls,
smudging snow, sky, air. The sun flickers, refuses to fade.
I am saying goodbye.

Evidence: While he wakes I walk the mountain: Hoarfrost—
tasting of sky and dust and cold—thickens as I climb.

Fetal (4 A.M.): I listened to the dark and to silence—
dark's beloved familiar—receding

and to him sleeping in the same soft sheets
in the close heated room.

I fingered the satin binding and thought:
Whatever is known about winter, I know,
have always known, will know better now.

On the day I leave, I leave the mountain
first. Early sun turns fuzz of frost to something slick.

SLOW CURVE, FALLING ROCK, PASSING LANE, the signs explain
in the light sharpening these things:

him refusing the window, me

already gone.

III.
THE MINOTAUR

The Day Beauty Divorced Meaning

Their friends looked shocked—said *not
possible,* said *how sad.* The trees carried on
with their treeish lives—stately except when
they shed their silly dandruff of birds. And
the ocean did what oceans mostly do—
suspended almost everything, dropped one
small ship, or two. The day beauty divorced
meaning, someone picked a flower, a fight,
a flight. Someone got on a boat.
A closet lost its suitcases. Someone
was snowed in, someone else on. The sun
went down and all it was, was night.

Past Tense

Was fired—on fire, not absent from pay
Was burning, was being fire over water
Was ashes, ashes. Was all fall down.
Was dusted was lusted. Was lusted after
Was flower'd. Not de- too late for that
Was leafed and green was left
Was left after—long—the altar
Was altered, leaning far out of true
Was pitched was pitched wrong, and also out.
Strung, instrument, was plucked
Was plucky, lucky, unlucky
Was—and was not—well, fucked.
Was well was water—not still but moving
Was moving down—not south, but lower
Was low in deed in thought in estimation—not numeric but regard.
Was indeed low.
Was estimated to be lost, have lost
Was judged marbleless—not Carrara but round and rolling—
Was gathering no moss
Was glass seen and also through. Scenery. Gawked at. A wreck.
Was broke. Was unbroken, unwept. Was swept—from field, not
    floor
Was fleet until was fled. Was well under sail
Was passed, past—was cast. Was cast out, flung. Not dice, but die—
Was suddenly singular, was thrown. Down and gauntlet gloved.
Was sheathed, sheaved, mown. Was pulled
Was pulled forward and also
Apart. Was a part of what? a pair? a pier? a plank?
Was walking the plank, was hiking—all back.

Was sad. Was said to be sadly lacking in sense. Was lacking
Exactly half—better? worse? For better or worse was naked,
Stripped clutched and was (again) pluck'd, unpetaled, all fallen.
    Was drop't.
Was he loves me. Is he loves me not.

Fifty States: A Travelogue (V)

Lost Socks

> Knickknacks and garden gnomes,
> antiromantic, where what is sundered,
> and modestly priced,
> is what endures.

Anthropomorphism: Yellowjacket

> Trapped, crackling like new fire,
> frantic in an old coffee tin,
> it is rage—all hissing buzz
> and exoskeletal ping.
> Or not rage, but fear or instinct
> or dumb insect confusion
> at first finding itself flown hard
> at a clarity it couldn't escape
> then left alone in a shining dark place.

Solid, Liquid, Gas

> White skin of ice, black hole
> of flesh, silver breath. We walk on water
> forever, drown only where it pools,
> grows warm.

Sadness

> Coastal, flat, prone to inundation,
> sudden helpless fits of weeping.

State bird: There is none, nothing flies here,
what was I thinking?

Hell

Everything speaks. And carries knives:
blades of grass, gutshot deer, discarded lovers,
garden flowers. At the border, your voice is taken;
they are waiting. Even the trellised wallpaper
to which you once tacked pictures of him
has something to say,
wants to talk about the pushpins.

Cause

One of the missing states,
ceded to history, treatied over
to beforeness — similar to yesterday,
but with more intent. As in

How can I be homesick
if I lack the proximate cause?

Loss

In summit light the night, the day,
each moment weighs itself, calculates.
Loss is a simple equation —
a question of long division.

Despair

This simple hollow sphere
is the state
of being perfected.
Annealed.
Enisled.

Cartography

State motto: Where the lost are found,
cross-referenced, indexed, bound.

Inventory

There is always a beloved.
Sometimes there is a husband.
The two were one so long ago that nobody remembers.
One of them you slept with.
Both are presumed lost.
There are several landscapes, a city, four towns,
one mountain, and every river that ever flowed.
One of the landscapes is briefly California.
All of the towns drowned before your birth.
There are two seasons: winter and not winter.

Pronouns are flex points in the narrative.
Sometimes the you is any one of two others.
Sometimes it is not exactly other.
He is also changeable.
I is sometimes I, but sometimes
its more prescient twin.

The rules involve the number of people, places, pronouns
acquired but not held.
When they are not full of stones, your pockets are empty.
When you believe you are being most direct
you are mistaken.
One of the twins has been known to lie, one writes some things
     down.
You love best that which cannot love in return.
This list of loves includes one of the landscapes,
the city, and at least one of the men.

There is always a beloved. Sometimes there is a husband.
There has never been a home.

The Maps

When I finished coming to California
I burned the maps at the edge
of this wrong sea,

the ash mingling with ash
already falling from fires suddenly *east.*

I needed a reason not to go back. No maps
was all I had. I also wanted—
the same old want—the outside to match

the inside: the hole I keep throwing
states into, the hole whose size

doesn't change, the one that looks
like a rearview mirror into which
everything first shrinks, then disappears.

I thought California might balance the ache.
It was a big state. I had to try.

Love — as memory

Any river carries the shapes of all the bodies
only so long as the bodies remain.

Remove flesh from river, let the divers
recover — and the river heals itself,

refuses to imagine the next one
who jumps or slips or is thrown —

In this way is a book like love: it will hold
the memory of the bodies — be infused, absolute.

Burn them, send the ash to fall from the sky
and still —

Ash arrives at the river and the river
makes way. The ash tastes of fire

and the river wonders about burning —
this thing it can see, but never have, never be.

Binary

In the presence of absence, ghosts become habitual—even breathing
begs failure.

When you leave a physical location, the substation silence
forwards all your mail.

There is always a way back into boxes, no good way
out of triangles.

You cannot discard evocative objects—
all objects evoke.

Boxes, like nations, are subject to division, geometry.

The disc is divisible into tracks your animal mind follows, instinctive
and starving.

If you follow the tracks across a geography of distance, you are not fed
but hunted.

All the music you possess is described by a binary sequence.

Every position is either one or none.

Winter

It was winter, that much I remember.
The light—it came from everywhere
except maybe the sky.

What the sky spat down into the woods was
sharp—each piece of dust tucked,
enfolded in the crystal.

How the snow or rain requires
that desert heart, or nothing grows,
nothing falls.

2.

It was not winter. If there had been
snow, I would have missed
the bones—they would have been

invisible in all that hard white light.

3.

It must have been winter or the opening—
low and on the wrist—would have bled.
Cold like ether, like a cudgel

is one type of amputation. I chose
a long splintered bone—head
like a fist, the entrywound prepared

the thrust, the way it fit—clean like crystal.
But its companions on the ground twitched
closer to order, closer to articulation,

closer to meaning.

4.

If it was not winter
where did all the light arise?
Why does every single tree resemble bones?

Why am I so cold?

5.

In this way I acquired a phantom limb. No.
Season?—No. *Beloved?*—No. I merely
reinforced the prison. Bone to bone I wed

myself and when I wake alone, lost
in the trees, the tangled sky, lost
in the fall of fractal-edged flakes

I give the bones permission to ache
for the ones separated, the ones
I left. My hands splay and twitch

for remembered, absent flesh. In my chest
the message grows confused and I cannot tell
what hurts: the cage I left,

the one I carry, or my idle bat-hung heart.

Maps

I buy by the dozen, stack next
to tea bags, dog food, next to

nights of no sleep when,
unfurling a new one, I mark

the places I've lived and draw—
a westward, erratic line

like a live heart stuttering
into fibrillation; the line

from most north—ragged
W's that doppler away

from winter, season of
my belonging; the random

lines that almost assemble
into image, carnage:

the one that draws the witch,
the one like hands broken

from a body, the great fish,
worn hills, stalled flock

of birds at scatter, water
in a riffle, a rifle, a gun—

I'm leaving again.

Fifty States: A Travelogue (VI)

Childhood

Where the government's
most often proffered gift
is something
to really make you cry.

Marriage

For me, like the world—
just another three-chambered heart.

Memory

Traitor's land. Prone to sudden
eruptions, elisions, dream sequences.
Operates under the rules
of quantum mechanics. You choose
particle or wave—the shore
or what covers it.

History

An implied narrative where I get
to say I fucked him (though this is
not true), where I say that I loved him.
Him and not you.

Animal

> *What do you do with a body*
> *this wild to be held?*

Mineral

> Tears are defined, in part,
> by a capacity to wash away
> foreign bodies.

Persistent Vegetative

> The long disconnect:
> mind cut away from body,
> body a plant in winter
> apprenticed to cold, re-leaved,
> relieved by sleep, by dreams,
> by damage.

Utility

> You were the kite I used
> to learn to love the wind.

How I Became a Ghost

It was all about objects, their objections
expressed through a certain solidity.

My house, for example, still moves
through me, moves me.
When I tried to reverse the process
I kept dropping things, kept finding myself
in the basement.

Windows became more than
usually problematic.
I wanted to break them,
which didn't work, though for a while

I had more success with the lake.

The phone worked for a long time
though when I answered
often nobody was there.

Bats crashed into me at night,
but then didn't anymore.

The rings vanished from my hand,
the pond.

I stopped feeling the wind.

One day the closets were empty.

Another day the mirrors were.

Book Report

If you are single, begin by describing the cover—
look and feel—texture, weight, the heft.

If married, tell the story of how the baby
drooled on the denouement.

If you are a tree, talk about the shredding—
stew of our mingled flesh.

If you are a scholar,
begin with the annunciation.

If you are a farmer, run your tongue across the ink;
the parent will find this most upsetting.

If you are an insect, use the crucial sex scene
to shore up your defenses.

If you are blind, tear and cast it into the stream.
Listen to the story the way the river tells it.

If you are the river, lie about the ending.

If you are the ocean, reassemble the fragments—
accost the octopus; gather its panic and ink and ire.

Let the vintner commission a wide-mouthed bottle.

Let the shipwrecked come back as the living—
find the bottle, a towel, the deck chair.

Let the decks rise dry beneath them.

Let them begin right there.

IV.

ICARUS

Self-Portrait as an Eastern Hardwood Forest

1.

This life begins with scene notes: dawnshine,
flat water, heron, the pine woods

> *Once a squirrel could cross ten states*
> *on a highway made of chestnut branches.*

and these (trees, water, sky, bird knitting it
all together) establish the parameters.

For most of part one you are the birds
rocking into and from the dark entanglements,

parabolic, native to season, not place.
Unlike the birds', your season has always been

winter, has never been light. What dead there were,
fell at the edges with the sound of empty bells.

> *A forest can keep, absent of even one*
> *leaf, a severed stump alive. For years.*

Humans slide their dead into ordered rows,
peel back the envelope of ground, lick it shut with blades.

2.

There will always be a line of men wanting
to transform you—sharp instruments, the plans

When the blight took hold, one tree of every four
withered, and a very specific shade of gold

they've made in which you are a featured
ingredient—spar, drawer, windowframe—

in which you are planed, dovetailed, offered
as sacrifice to the god of his strong house.

vanished from the world.

3.

Your sister's fiancé, whom she later
marries anyway, catches you

outside at night. First kiss, first lesson:
all that betrayal requires

Believing the trees were doomed, men
rushed to harvest what was as yet unfallen.

is being alive. After, you notice the gaps
between trees, the flicker of shadow,

the growth of immigrant white pines—
newly born body parts—untrustworthy and strange.

4.

You fall in love with one river, spend years
believing it can be saved. You notice the

orchards planted in open glades, the deer,
their skittish reach, longing for fruit—

> *Some chestnuts were naturally blight resistant*
> *but enough were ill, were cut*

Sometimes fire sometimes knives
sometimes hunger—a kind of blight—

and holes form, hollows, absences
of a very specific sort:

> *that the species, as a whole,*
> *could not be saved*

so much of you is missing, has been transformed,
amputated, covered over

in strangers, you begin to practice longing
(migration) as a form of prayer.

5.

There is virtually no old growth left

> *but it is not extinct*

Instructions to the Realtor

All windows must be mullioned, old,
the glass thicker at the bottom,
rippled, not necessarily intact.

You want the views to be
most clearly that—the outside confined
by careful edges, patient trim.

Nothing sharp, nothing a body
can be tied to. No easy access,
except for bats welcome in the attic.

No armchairs, table legs, Depression glass,
no cedar shakes, spalted wood, antiques—
nothing that implies a narrative.

Every part—nails, stair, clapboards, and rafters
must be gathered from somewhere else,
somewhere dismantled or destroyed.

There must be a river nearby,
no mice, no cellar, few neighbors
far north—pitched roof,

an island in the kitchen, a moat,
a gate. All doors must be weathered,
off true, the locks sturdy and absolute.

Fifty States: A Travelogue (VII)

The Moon

I love the moon
for battered, for barren, for shine
despite an utter absence
of capacity for light.

Sound

It was bright, dark; I didn't wake, sleep—
dreamed. I sang small fish and creeks,
mist and glitter.
Here the sun—hear the sun not singing, on fire—
fighting patrol. No caddisflies, no rise.

All that time dreaming and awake
all that singing—I still don't know
what he heard in the air, the ink.

Garden

The discontinuity is this:
inside, I am all angles, sand. Once
I felt it shift, sift through, resettle. Once
it was larger—gravel, small pebbles,
stones. The edges fracture and I hiss,
whisper like small bells without
tongue. I garden, not for the growing,
but for the broken and the dead
from which they come.

Migration

White walls, wingfeathers dipped
in ink and October,
no window, indication
just the frantic calligraphy
in a south-facing corner—
paint marked by the inevitable
as though what any one thing wants
matters.

Love —as senility

The old man who lives in the high-rise
on St. Paul and often tries to sell his pants
says he only ever sees blondes at 8 A.M.

I ask him where we go the rest of the time.
And what he says, around his cigarette
and the thrum of downtown buses,

and across the hood of my car aimed
once more north, what he says is
Don't worry. You will fall in love again.

Fifty States: A Travelogue (VIII)

Practice

It isn't so much that I can't
let him go as that I need
to do it over and over again—
lose him every single way
he can be lost.

Topiary

Sometimes I want
to take hedge-trimmers to my soul,
carve it into some recognizable shape—snail,
or rabbit, maybe apple, giraffe—
anything to make it stop
wearing my heart like a bracelet.

Sewing

I keep stitching you back
into silence—crude black sutures
threaded through your lips.

No wind, no matter how cold, how far blown,
has ever howled for me the way
your body does the way your voice does
through the black lines sewing up
a thousand miles of bad roads.
Please stop calling.

For my house, a song of gratitude

All houses speak, but this had lived with absence
a long time. Empty and scarred with rotten
sills and rippled windows, it was being
consumed by those who come to fill the void:

the rats and ants and the darker ones, the ones
who do not so much fill the space as deepen it—
subterranean hordes that hum with what feels
like hate. Weeds and glass shards litter the yard.

Behind the shallow abandoned well lie tumbled
rectangles—chimney someone sledgehammered
into rubble, but rubble with a hole
at the center where its purpose used to be.

All houses speak, but this one wept. I sing
for a sadness equal to my own, and the good
bones crumbling, for the empty spaces
the walls surround, and for the lake next door

that fills and empties then fills again—with rain
and mist, with geese and kayaks—for these and for
the granite hours when all that moved through both
of us was the shallow light of afternoon

sinking down, coming back again.

Music — as infection

You might as well stay
is what the dead say, even though

it is spring—season of stinging, and
exploding exponential green,

even though the things the living acquire
include surgeons and all that they imply,

even though your life is full
of boxes and broken frames and

singing, persistent rivers that keep

reflecting and taking, easing
objects down and downstream,

even though you fear love, love grief.

All that is left to the dead
is the watery shine

of the stone headboards
marking their last rectangles

and these, their spinning, remaindered songs.
They are the ghosts in this particular machine

singing of all they lost until all was lost
except this last ability to infect the living.

Tea

Nearly dawn, I'm watching the trees
march out of night, surround again
this house; the dogs

twitch in final dreams; the stove —
this orange, unsteady heat and black iron box

breathes warm mirage into the cold,
into the sky; the yellow enamel teapot
does the same inside.

The tea leaves in their white paper pouch
in their skyblue mug — I've brewed thousands of cups

like this: wood house, wood fire, the woods
leaning out of the night, of their stubborn life,

the taste of leaves
hot on my tongue.

Pantoum for a Walk in the Woods

Everything rhymes. Take a forest of trees,
thousands (each different, but they are lost
in the crowd), and rocks uncounted, a host of bees
in a standing snag. Walking, I pass them all

by the thousands. Each difference is lost:
too many, so nearly the same. They rhyme, but
stand together, snagging meaning, leaving it all
to repeat, endlessly. Differences, so small,

are nearly the same. The rhythm of walking
follows the contour of the climb, and the heart
repeats, endlessly. Diffident, its small
stutter is locked to quiet. This pattern

follows the cadence of the climb. The heart
contrives with breath; the eyes refuse all difference,
become locked, in step with the quiet stutter
of stones underfoot. And the miles go by,

contriving with the body to refuse all distances.
I remember the crowded, cluttered wealth
of stones underfoot. And the miles go by
like giants, self-referential, meaningless.

I remember the crowded, cluttered woods,
the lumbering grace of the mysterious other—
like giants, self-referential—all meaning
hidden in the difference. We move through life

in the crowd, uncounted, a thousand bees
hiding and hidden. In our different lives,
nothing rhymes. And we mistake the trees
for each other, for lumber, or for pews.

House Cool from the Night—

high clear sky promising heat later dustbird

its barely twitched wings the mayapples neon white

the humming bees the rhody the dark sentinel trees

carries all of it me out into the day with two muses dogs

the ones who lick and love and keep me keep me please

in this world when today so many days there is no single person

anywhere everywhere who knows where knows how the morning
carries me

to the deep lake past redtails and whitetails and unceasing green
movement

decorating the edges as wind does the surface as sky does the
surface

as shadows decorate surface and depth while the center remains

empty inaccessible carries me from the last house

before deep water full of sleep and night

left for the sky the hike the going

and the hope of coming back

Lately I Have Been Dark and at Peace

Is it better to resist essential nature or learn to dwell within

once upon a time I loved once I married a man loved another

once I turned the snow's shallow acknowledgments to wings

a frozen lake to dusk and glide I do not love the dark the cold

for death for barren or despair I never needed to learn to love

the winter the water the world absent us and our busy makings

I loved them for extreme for all edges apparent for indifference

to my losses to loss that already includes both men for knives

and utility and danger for not pretending the universe

is kind for true things made more accessible for indivisible

the cleave from the shine

Notes

"Farming the Moon," page 29: With no atmosphere to protect it, the moon is constantly barraged by meteors. These impacts break the rock that composes the moon's surface into ever finer particles. Some scientists refer to this as farming the moon. I first heard this phrase on a radio show.

"Instructions to the Realtor," page 68: Spalted wood refers to wood in the early stages of a specific kind of decay. A fungus called white rot invades the wood, leaving dark streaks that look like woodgrain. These streaks are said to form lines of demarcation between incompatible fungus colonies. Most common and most beautiful in pale hardwoods such as birch, beech, and maple, this figured wood is prized by woodworkers.

"Fifty States: A Travelogue (VII)," page 69: The section called "Migration" refers to scientists' use of a device called an Emlen funnel—a white inverted cone with an inkpad at the bottom. A migratory bird is placed on the inkpad, and scientists study the ink markings on the sides of the cone to better understand migratory instincts.

Acknowledgments

My sincere gratitude to the editors of the following journals in which these poems, some in slightly altered form, first appeared. My thanks to all who read, subscribe to, and support these journals.

Barn Owl Review: "How It Started"
Burnside Review: "The Maps"
diode: "Huntley Meadows, May"; "Winter"; "Home —as hiking"; "Maps"
Memorious: "Love —as memory"; "How I Became a Ghost"
New Republic: "Autobiography —as a vase"
Ninth Letter: "Binary"
Orion: "Tea"
Poetry: "The Four Elements"; "Pantoum for a Walk in the Woods"
Pool: "Inventory"; "The Day Beauty Divorced Meaning"
Sewanee Theological Review: "A Thousand Miles"; "Solstice"
Solo: A Journal of Poetry: "Fragments —on hiking"

My endless gratitude to my teachers, especially Tom Sleigh, Allen Grossman, Jim McMichael, and Michael Ryan.

To my classmates, friends, colleagues, and trusted readers on both coasts and many places in between, especially Amelia, Gae, Greg, Grier, Hallie, Jehanne, Jen, Katrina, Lisa, Matt, and Morgan—my profound gratitude for your care, wisdom, courage, friendship, and humor always.

Boundless thanks to Eavan Boland for finding something here, and Michael Collier for kindness, patience, presence, guidance, and astonishing generosity. And thanks to all the people at Houghton Mifflin Harcourt, especially Elizabeth Lee, Susanna Brougham, Melissa Lotfy, Meagan Stacey, Lena Williams, and Loren Foye.

Last but never far from my thoughts (and so these pages) are two people without whom this book would simply not exist—Sasha West and Greg Williamson.

Bread Loaf and the Bakeless Prizes

The Katharine Bakeless Nason Literary Publication Prizes were established in 1995 to expand the Bread Loaf Writers' Conference's commitment to the support of emerging writers. Endowed by the LZ Francis Foundation, the prizes commemorate Middlebury College patron Katharine Bakeless Nason and launch the publication career of a poet, a fiction writer, and a creative nonfiction writer annually. Winning manuscripts are chosen in an open national competition by a distinguished judge in each genre. Winners are published by Houghton Mifflin Harcourt Publishing Company in Mariner paperback original.

2008 Judges
•

Antonya Nelson
Fiction

Tom Bissell
Nonfiction

Eavan Boland
Poetry